APR 0 4 2007

HORSEPOWER

JETS

by Carrie A. Braulick

Reading Consultant:
Barbara J. Fox
Reading Specialist
North Carolina State University

Capstone
press®

Mankato, Minnesota

Blazers is published by Capstone Press,
151 Good Counsel Drive, P.O. Box 669, Mankato, Minnesota 56002.
www.capstonepress.com

Library of Congress Cataloging-in-Publication Data
Braulick, Carrie A., 1975–
    Jets / by Carrie A. Braulick.
    p. cm.—(Blazers. Horsepower)
    Summary: "Simple text and photographs describe jets, their
design and uses"—Provided by publisher.
    Includes bibliographical references and index.
    ISBN-13: 978-0-7368-6451-0 (hardcover)
    ISBN-10: 0-7368-6451-2 (hardcover)
    1. Jet planes—Juvenile literature. I. Title. II. Series.
TL547.B738 2007
629.133'349—dc22   2006001010

Editorial Credits
Sarah L. Schuette, editor; Jason Knudson, set designer;
    Thomas Emery, book designer; Jo Miller, photo researcher;
    Scott Thoms, photo editor

Photo Credits
AirShows America, 5
Check Six/George Hall, 22–23
Corbis/George Hall, cover; Philip Wallick, 28–29
DVIC/TSGT Michael Haggerty, 13 (top)
Getty Images Inc./AFP/Lousia Gouliamaki, 26; Boeing, 17; Joe McNally,
    25; Mladen Antonov, 27
Glenn Grossman, 6, 7 (both), 8, 9
NASA Dryden Flight Research Center, 13 (bottom)
Ted Carlson/Fotodynamics, 12, 21 (both)
U.S. Air Force/Master Sgt. Thomas Meneguin, 18; Staff Sgt. James
    Wilkinson, 19
U.S. Navy/PHAA Nathan Laird, 11; PH2 Ryan J. Courtade, 20; PH3
    Barbara Snider, 15; PH3 Kristopher Wilson, 14

**Blazers thanks Raymond L. Puffer, PhD, Historian at Edwards AFB, for his
assistance with this book.**

1 2 3 4 5 6 11 10 09 08 07 06

TABLE OF CONTENTS

WHAT A SHOW!

A team of jets climbs into the air. Their engines whine. The crowd gasps as the Patriots begin the show.

Suddenly, the jets zoom in
different directions. They roll
sideways, forming loops in the sky.
Flying back together, they make
a pattern.

Seconds later, the jets glide down
to the ground. The crowd rushes to
get autographs from their favorite
pilots. What a show!

BLAZER FACT

The maximum speed of a Patriot jet is 560 miles (900 kilometers) per hour.

POINTED AND POWERFUL

Jet planes have powerful engines that burn a mixture of air and fuel. Exhaust rushes out of the engines, pushing the planes forward.

Pointed noses and swept-back
tails help jets slice through the air.
Tails help keep planes steady.

BLAZER FACT

Jets without tails are just as easy to control as jets with tails.

F/A-18 Hornet

Sometimes flying fast isn't quite fast enough. An afterburner creates an added burst of speed. To use the afterburner, pilots press a button in the cockpit.

BLAZER FACT

Afterburners need to be inspected often to make sure they are working correctly.

JETS OF ALL KINDS

Jets have many jobs. A jet's design depends on its uses. Huge passenger jets carry people. The famous Boeing 737 holds about 190 passengers.

F-15 Strike Eagle

Fast, powerful U.S. military jets
are a threat to enemies everywhere.
The F-15 is the fastest military jet.
It flies 1,875 miles (3,000 kilometers)
per hour.

The huge C-5 Galaxy jet can carry equipment weighing 270,000 pounds (122,500 kilograms).

C-5 Galaxy

AIR MOBILITY COMMAND

Blue Angels

Aerobatic jets perform amazing stunts in the sky. The jets fly so close together, they look like they are touching. Trails of smoke mark the jets' path.

Blue Angels

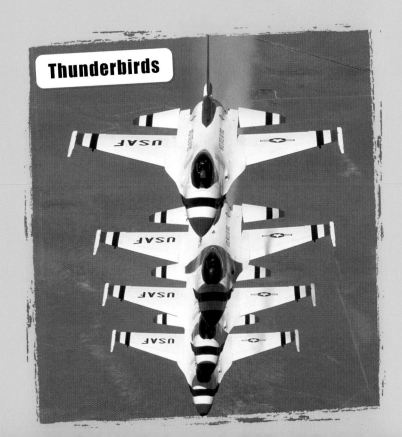

Thunderbirds

JET PARTS

Cockpit

Engine

Wing

Tail

EYES TO THE SKY!

Jets are all about speed, and pilots want to prove it. Fast loops, dives, and rolls thrill crowds at air shows.

Flying in formation, carrying passengers, or racing to battle, it doesn't matter what job jets have. Their roaring engines overhead will draw your eyes to the sky!

GLOSSARY

afterburner (AF-tur-bur-nur)—the part of a jet engine that burns extra fuel to create more power

cockpit (KOK-pit)—the area in the front of a jet where the pilot sits; pilots control a jet's movement with controls in the cockpit.

engine (EN-juhn)—a machine where fuel burns to provide power to a jet

exhaust (eg-ZAWST)—the heated gases that leave a jet engine

READ MORE

Clemson, Wendy. *Using Math to Fly a Jumbo Jet.* Mathworks! Milwaukee: Gareth Stevens, 2005.

Hansen, Ole Steen. *The AV-8B Harrier Jump Jet.* Cross-sections. Mankato, Minn.: Capstone Press, 2005.

Roza, Greg. *The Incredible Story of Jets.* A Kid's Guide to Incredible Technology. New York: PowerKids Press, 2004.

INTERNET SITES

FactHound offers a safe, fun way to find Internet sites related to this book. All of the sites on FactHound have been researched by our staff.

Here's how:

1. Visit *www.facthound.com*

2. Choose your grade level.

3. Type in this book ID **0736864512** for age-appropriate sites. You may also browse subjects by clicking on letters, or by clicking on pictures and words.

4. Click on the **Fetch It** button.

FactHound will fetch the best sites for you!

INDEX